FAITH

— AND —

FINANCES

ETERNAL PROMISES FOR
TODAY'S RESOURCES

D0981707

TIM ROSEN

First published in 2014 by Striving Together Publications, a ministry
of Lancaster Baptist Church, Lancaster, CA 93535. Striving Together
Publications is committed to providing tried, trusted, and proven
resources that will further equip local churches to carry out the
Great Commission. Your comments and suggestions are valued.

Striving Together Publications
4020 E. Lancaster Blvd.
Lancaster, CA 93535
800.201.7748
www.strivingtogether.com

Cover design by Andrew Jones
Layout by Craig Parker
Edited by Rob Byers
Special thanks to our proofreaders

The author and publication team have put forth every effort to give proper
credit to quotes and thoughts that are not original with the author. It is not
our intent to claim originality with any quote or thought that could not
readily be tied to an original source.

ISBN 978-1-59894-264-4
Printed in the United States of America

Contents

Introduction

You've heard it said: "Money makes the world go 'round." In truth, money is woven into every part of life. As long as we live, we will be dealing with money—how to get it, how to spend it, how to save it, and how to give it.

The world bombards us with conflicting messages regarding money. And most of those messages are in contradiction to the Word of God.

The world tells us, for instance, that he who dies with the most toys wins, but time and again we see people who have plenty of toys taking their own lives as they realize the emptiness of possessions.

The world system promotes loving and trusting money, while offering no real solution for money-related worry and stress. And Christians are certainly not immune to the allure of money. Why do so many Christians struggle with money? God has given us the freedom to choose, and all too often we choose the world's philosophy of money rather than God's commandments.

If you do a Google search for "how to manage money" you will get hundreds of millions of results. It would take many lifetimes to read them all—yet most of them are filled with advice that contradicts God's directives on our money. If we want the same results the world is experiencing, we can simply follow the world's advice. If, however, we desire the benefits that God has planned for us, we must turn to His wisdom and follow His guidance.

The Bible reminds us, "For my thoughts are not your thoughts, Neither are your ways my ways, saith the Lord"(Isaiah 55:8). Further we read, "There is a way that seemeth right unto a man, but the end thereof are the ways of death" (Proverbs 16:25). When we take an honest look at our ways and compare them to God's way, we see they are very different. When we follow God's way, we can experience the peace of the promises God has for us.

The goal of this book is to point you to the many precious, but overlooked or under-applied, promises in God's Word related to our finances. It is to show you that these principles could and should be embraced to help you be equipped to do more for the Kingdom of God. Following God's principles will strengthen both your relationships and your testimony, and it will enable you to experience peace and joy in your finances.

While you may be tempted to skip ahead to the chapters that deal with particular issues you are facing right now, I encourage you to read from the beginning to the end. Before we get to the practical "how to" sections, we need to lay a scriptural foundation concerning God's view of money. The best way to achieve lasting results is to learn and embrace biblical truth and then draw practical applications from that. So let's see what God says about money.

Chapter One
A Matter of the Heart

Many Christians assume that money is a matter of budgets and spreadsheets, income and expenses. They think of it strictly in terms of material or emotional benefits and results.

But Scripture teaches us that money is, first and foremost, a matter of the heart. There are over two thousand verses that address money, and sixteen of the thirty-eight parables taught by Christ deal with money and possessions.

Why is much of the Bible dedicated to this subject? God knows how challenging it is for us to rightly deal with money, so He gave us His wisdom to help us avoid tragedy and achieve success.

Consider the rich young ruler who asked Christ how to obtain eternal life. Jesus replied, "...go and sell that thou hast, and give to the poor, and thou shalt have treasure in heaven: and come and follow me" (Matthew 19:21). Why did Christ make this command? Why not simply, "Trust Me as your Saviour?" Jesus knew the young man's heart—specifically what was on the throne of his heart. Christ's command exposed the sinful love of money and possessions of the man's heart. But rather than repent and place his trust in Christ, the rich young ruler turned and left sorrowfully. He would not part with his riches—they had a grip on his *heart*.

Contrast the young ruler's sad story with that of another rich man who met Jesus. This man didn't just meet Him, he "sought to see Jesus who he was..." and "...ran before, and climbed up into a sycamore tree to see him..." (Luke 19:3-4). Zacchaeus was a publican—a tax collector for the Romans. The Roman system allowed its collectors to keep everything they received over a set quota, so publicans wrung every possible penny out of the people. Understandably, they were despised among the common people.

Yet, despite his greedy, compassionless ways, Zaccheaus was still a soul that God loved, and Jesus called him out of the tree by name. When Zaccheus met Jesus face to face, the first words out of his mouth were, "Behold, Lord, the half of my goods I give to the poor; and if I have taken any thing from any man by false accusation, I restore him fourfold" (Luke 19:8).

Notice the contrast: Jesus did not instruct this rich man to sell all he had and give to the poor, as He told the other rich man. What made the difference? Zaccheus' voluntary offer was an outward expression of the inward change in his heart. He no longer loved wealth; he loved the Saviour!

While we should be following the example of Zaccheus, many Christians are living more like the rich young ruler—we love wealth rather than the Saviour. Paul warned Timothy (and us): "But they that will be rich fall into temptation and a snare, and into many foolish and hurtful lusts, which drown men in destruction and perdition. For the love of money is the root of all evil: which while some coveted after, they have erred from the faith, and pierced themselves through with many sorrows" (1 Timothy 6:9–10).

The phrase "the love of money" indicates the reality that money is too easily given a place—not just in our wallets or budgets, but in our *hearts*. One of the meanings of the word *err* is to "be seduced," and isn't that an appropriate term to describe the alluring pull of money? If we are to have peace, joy, and a sound mind in relation to our finances, we need to align our hearts with God's Word. We cannot cling to God's promises while excluding from our practices the principles related to money. Our faith and our finances cannot be divorced.

Can we trust God's Word to teach, instruct, correct, comfort and guide us in this very important, and often, personal, area of money?

We can. Let's discover how.

Chapter Two
The Truth of Ownership

We must never forget that we are in a spiritual war. We have an enemy who attacks on many fronts. One of the fiercest spiritual battles for the Christian is in the area of finances and possessions. The enemy's attacks are not necessarily blatantly obvious, like tempting us to rob a bank. Usually, Satan tempts most Christians subtly. Perhaps it's an argument with our spouse over spending, the feeling of jealousy because a friend bought a newer, fancier car than ours, or a lack of gratitude for what God has already blessed us with.

If the devil can get us to focus on worrying about money or loving an abundance of wealth, he succeeds in getting us to take our eyes off the Lord. His ultimate goal is to harm the name of Jesus. In Hosea 13:6 we read that the children of Israel "were filled, and their heart was exalted; therefore have they forgotten me." Satan wants to render your life ineffective for the cause of Christ, and one way he attacks is through your money. He wants you to believe the subtle lie that you own it all—that you are in charge. He wants your money to conquer you.

And yet, this is directly opposite what God's Word teaches us. Notice these three principles that give us freedom from the hold money can have on our hearts.

God is the ultimate owner of all things.

The earth is the Lord's, and the fullness thereof; the world, and they that dwell therein.—PSALM 24:1

God owns the earth by right of creation. He made everything, and it all belongs to Him. We see His hand of creation everywhere we look. We can see the miracles of His creation daily in the rising and setting of the sun, in our hearts that beat without a conscious effort, and in our ability to fight off germs and viruses that attack.

Not only is God the Creator, but He is also the caretaker. God takes very good care of *all* that is His!

He takes care of the world. God set the earth spinning on its axis at 1,040 miles per hour—a perfect speed. If it were spinning any faster, the centrifugal force would send us flying into space. He placed the earth 92,960,000 miles from the sun. If it were any closer, we would burn from the heat; if it were any further away we would freeze.

God takes care of nature. I read a recent estimate that there are over 10,500 species of birds, with new species being discovered every year.[1] Why so many? God displays His awesome power of creation and care for His creation. He takes care of the birds—every member of all 10,500 species.

Jesus made a connection between God taking care of creation and His care for us:

> Behold the fowls of the air: for they sow not, neither do they reap, nor gather into barns; yet your heavenly Father feedeth them. Are ye not much better than they? Which of you by taking thought can add one cubit unto his stature? And why take ye thought for raiment? Consider the lilies of the field, how they grow; they toil not, neither do they spin: And yet I say unto you, That even Solomon in all his glory was not arrayed like one

---

1   Frank Gill and David Donsker (Editors), *IOC World Bird List (version 4.1)*, 2014.

of these. Wherefore, if God so clothe the grass of the field,
which to day is, and to morrow is cast into the oven,
shall he not much more clothe you, O ye of little faith?
— MATTHEW 6:26–30

If God cares for the world He made and everything in it, He will surely care for us as well. He is more than able and willing to take care of you and meet your needs.

We belong to God.

For ye are bought with a price: therefore glorify God
in your body, and in your spirit, which are God's.
—1 CORINTHIANS 6:20

God owns the earth by right of creation, but we are doubly owned by God. Not only did He create us, but He also redeemed us. If you've trusted Christ as your Saviour, you belong to God—purchased by the blood of Christ.

The fact that God doubly owns us should be a relief to us. It means He will provide for us. It means the care of provision is His—much like a father provides for his children.

Yet, Satan, ever seeking to turn our trust from God, whispers in our ears that if we acknowledge that God owns everything—our jobs, our resources, our homes, our families, even our lives—He may take those things from us. And once he has us convinced that we must protect ourselves from God, he then seeks to consume our minds with the worry of being our own provider.

God's way is far simpler. When we acknowledge that our loving Heavenly Father owns and provides for us, we are freed from the cares of worry for tomorrow, and we are free to trust Him for what He does in our lives today.

Acknowledging God as our owner, however, is more than a simple admission of truth. It is surrender. Charles Spurgeon wisely said, "We want personal consecration. I have heard that word pronounced 'purse-and-all consecration,' a most excellent pronunciation certainly. He who loves Jesus consecrates to Him all that he has, and feels it a delight that he may lay anything at the feet of Him who laid down his life for us."

Our natural inclination is to view our needs—and what we perceive to be our needs for tomorrow—as if we are the owner. We bear the burdens of provision and success upon our own shoulders. We strive with matters of money, work, family and health because we do not see how the situation can improve.

We are not unlike the children of Israel who, though God miraculously delivered them from slavery in Egypt, quickly began worrying about food, water, clothing, and comfort. It was not long before they created something that they could see, putting their trust in and ascribing worth to an idol—the golden calf (Exodus 32:1–4).

We tend to live by sight rather than by faith, especially in the area of finances. I wish to challenge you through this book to radically change your perspective on money…and as a result experience the joy and peace and blessings that God has intended for you through claiming His promises.

The owner carries the burden, not the manager.

During the late eighties and early nineties, I worked as the manager of a jewelry store. In addition to hiring and training employees, I was responsible for protecting and tracking the inventory, which contained gold and diamonds valued at millions of dollars. I did not have to figure out on my own how to handle everything that might come up. The company had a *Policies and Procedures Manual*, which told me how to safely and efficiently manage the store, work with the employees, and keep the inventory safe. If I ignored the manual and did what I thought was best, the store could easily lose profits, employees, and possibly inventory.

From time to time the company would request that I send back to them certain valuable items, like diamond rings. When this happened, I would not throw up my hands and cry, "Why? Oh, why?" Those were not my items. I was entrusted with their care, but they did not belong to me. I would obediently send them back to the company—the real owner.

When we consciously acknowledge God's ownership and with all our hearts *give* Him all the precious things in our life, our burden is lifted. We are His managers, called to be faithful stewards, and He gladly bears the burden for us! Since God owns our lives, He also owns our trials, our concerns, and our problems. The great news is, we get to give it all to Jesus! That's how He works!

First Peter 5:7 says, "Casting all your care upon him; for he careth for you." When we are free from our burdens, having cast them upon the Lord, we are free to fully serve Him. Picture yourself carrying heavy packages, stacked on one another, reaching almost to the ceiling. It's hard to see where you are going, and there is a good chance you may stumble—but you don't want to let them go. Now picture handing them all to the Lord, who lovingly takes them and cares for them better than you can. Your muscles were so sore, you were getting weary, but now all the weight is suddenly gone. Your strength is back, your vision is clear, and now your arms and hands are free. What a relief!

Do you see the benefits of embracing the truth that God owns you? God's purpose is to be glorified *through* us. You see, He owns your victories also! As God works in your life, bearing your burdens, providing for you, and answering your prayers, He doesn't want you to keep it a secret! He desires your praise and that you would give him the glory and tell others of the great things He has done. Jesus told His disciples, "And whatsoever ye shall ask in my name, that will I do, that the Father may be glorified in the Son" (John 14:13).

The truth of ownership is one of the most liberating truths in Scripture. It frees us from the burden of being our own provider, and it frees us to approach our finances with an eternal perspective—managing God's money for Him.

But how are we to do it? That is the subject of our next chapter.

Chapter Three
Principles for Stewardship

When we say the Christian life is a journey, it is not a random hike through hills and valleys. Rather it is a carefully mapped out trek by the Creator Himself. Long before you were born, He had marvelous plans for you. David wrote, "…in thy book all my members were written, which in continuance were fashioned, when as yet there was none of them" (Psalm 139:16). The one who hung the stars in the heavens and has called them by name, knows *your* name and promises to be with you always.

Not only that, but God fills your life with good things. James wrote, "Every good gift and every perfect gift is from above, and cometh down from the Father of lights,

with whom is no variableness, neither shadow of turning"
(James 1:17).

God doesn't lavish these gifts on us because we deserve
them. Romans 3:10–12 provides an accurate portrayal of our
sinfulness: "As it is written, There is none righteous, no, not
one: There is none that understandeth, there is none that
seeketh after God. They are all gone out of the way, they
are together become unprofitable; there is none that doeth
good, no, not one."

It is absolutely awe-inspiring that a holy God would
not only pardon and forgive sinners such as you and I but
also bestow on us such incredible gifts. He gives so much
because of His great love for us.

As we have already seen, God calls us to steward—or
manage—the resources He has entrusted to us for Him.
First Corinthians 4:2 tells us the primary requirement of
stewardship: "Moreover it is required in stewards, that a
man be found faithful."

Let's take a look at this word *steward*. Webster's
Dictionary defines it as, "a person who manages another's
property or financial affairs; one who administers anything
as the agent of another or others."[1]

---

1   Dictionary.com (Random House, Inc., accessed April, 2014),
     http://dictionary.reference.com/browse/steward.

Just as the jewelry store gave me a *Policies and Procedures Manual*, God has given us a Steward's Manual—the Bible. If we follow what it says, we will be faithful to care for what He has entrusted to us.

To this point, we've seen that God owns everything—including us, our hearts, and our finances. We've seen that God wants to use us to accomplish His will and that He entrusts us with wonderful abilities and substance which we are to faithfully steward—or manage—for Him. Now, *how* do we steward His resources faithfully? Specifically, what does the Word of God say about how we should manage the money with which God has entrusted to our care?

Honoring the Lord with our substance

God wants us to put Him first, completely depending on Him alone. Proverbs 3:5–6 says, "Trust in the Lord with all thine heart; and lean not unto thine own understanding. In all thy ways acknowledge him, and he shall direct thy paths." What a comforting, timeless truth! God offers us direction in every area of life, including our money, when we acknowledge Him—doing what He says rather than what we think is right.

Just a few verses on, we find another timeless and encouraging promise of God's provision for us that is conditional upon a specific action on our part. Proverbs 3:9–10 says, "Honour the LORD with thy substance, and with the firstfruits of all thine increase: So shall thy barns be filled with plenty, and thy presses shall burst out with new wine." Of course, today most of us don't have barns and vats, but the principle applies in our modern economy. The means by which we make our living will be blessed if we are faithful to first honor God with our money.

Notice the order of this promise. Before we receive God's approval and blessing on our finances, we must first honor Him with the firstfruits of what He has entrusted to us. Many well-intended Christians get to the end of the month, having paid all the bills and put food on the table only to find that there is nothing left to give to God. It's not that they would not be willing to tithe, but that they pay their bills first. But God commands us to give to Him first. This is an act of faith, believing that He will provide for what we need.

Giving to the Lord is the first step in faithful stewardship, yet this is the point where many Christians put the "ownership hat" back on, and set aside the "manager's hat." They worry and fear that there will not be enough, and so they stop giving.

People have unlimited excuses for why they will not give to God first, but it comes down to what we believe most. Do we believe earthly wisdom, or God's promises? God does not need our money, but we need to receive what God wants to do in our lives as a result of our giving!

Beyond our understanding

God wants to work mightily on our behalf. However we cannot see Him do the impossible unless we exercise faith. Romans 1:17 tells us, "…The just shall live by faith," and Hebrews 11:6 reminds, "But without faith it is impossible to please him…." This is definitely true when it comes to giving. If we do not believe God's promises that He will meet all of our needs, we will hoard what we have rather than give. We can succumb to fear and miss out on amazing promises, or we can trust God completely and in the process become stronger in faith.

Think of the story of the widow in Zarephath found in 1 Kings 17. During a great famine, God sent His prophet Elijah there for food. When Elijah arrived, the widow told him she only had enough food for one last meal for herself and her son. In fact, she said she was getting two sticks to make a fire for that last meal. I don't know if you have ever built a fire or not, but two sticks isn't much wood!

Now imagine someone in that desperate situation being told to give food to someone else before her own son! Yet when Elijah told her that God would provide if she would obey, she believed. As evidence of that belief, she acted on what she was told. By faith, the widow obeyed. The result? Both she and her son ate for many days, and God received glory!

Many of our problems and struggles that are financial in nature would be solved if we would only trust God and follow His plan. Remember, "There is a way which seemeth right unto a man, but the end thereof are the ways of death" (Proverbs 14:12). Left to our own wisdom, our default mode is to operate by sight. That hinders the incredible work that God wants to do in our lives if we will just take His Word by faith.

God's provision for His purpose

Over and over in Scripture, God promises to provide for our needs as we give. One of these promises is 2 Corinthians 9:10: "Now he that ministereth seed to the sower both minister bread for your food, and multiply your seed sown, and increase the fruits of your righteousness."

There are some amazing truths about our finances packed into this one verse. We see that it is God who provides resources to believers, who then have the resources to give back to the Lord through offerings and giving to those in need. God promises to meet our needs, including the food for us to eat and clothing for us to wear. However, He does more than just the minimum—He replenishes our resources, providing us with even more to give. When we give back what He gives to us, we are blessed, those who are touched by our gifts are blessed, credit is placed on our eternal account, and God is pleased.

Based on the promises of God, we have no valid reason to believe that we cannot give to Him, or that our own needs will not be met if we give. Living according to God's will requires faith. The question is whether our faith is strong enough to face the test of doing what God says, even when we do not see how things will work out.

Evangelist Tom Farrell shared this personal story of how God works through those desiring to give: "At the end of 2011, our offerings were down because of the financial crunch nationwide. I told my wife that we were going to give more, not less, even in the down financial times. She agreed. The day I increased the offering and mailed out the check, a man was led of God to send our ministry an end-of-year offering for three times as much as I gave."

Luke 6:38 says, "Give, and it shall be given unto you." God is not restricted by recessions, job losses, or downturns in the economy. He has all the resources necessary to meet every need. The blessing He wants to bestow on us is only restricted by our lack of faith.

Pick up your sword!

There are many promises of God related to finances and His provision for us. He is faithful and will always be true to His promises. But God's promises require *faith* and *action* on our part. We cannot simply put our hands out and say, "Gimme!"

For example, God promised the children of Israel an inheritance, "…good land and a large, unto a land flowing with milk and honey…" (Exodus 3:8). But they could not simply arrive at that place, drive their family flag into the ground and announce, "I claim this property for the tribe of Benjamin!" They first had to drive out the inhabitants. God promised to deliver the inhabitants into their hands, but they still needed to suit up, put their armor on, pick up their sword and start fighting!

In Joshua 11:11 we read, "And they smote all the souls that were therein with the edge of the sword, utterly destroying them: there was not any left to breathe…." Receiving the land required *faith* and *action*, and the Lord honored both—He did as He promised.

Just as it requires faith to step into battle, it requires faith to obey God's Word in honoring Him financially. Putting on heavy armor and going to war requires getting out of the comfort zone. Giving liberally as God guides means getting out of our comfort zone! It requires discipline and effort to obey.

Occupy until I come

One of the many parables Jesus taught that deal with money and resources is the story of a nobleman who leaves a sum of money—one pound—entrusted to each of his servants before he goes on a journey. They do not know how long he will be gone, they are just told to be busy and productive with what they have been given.

One servant, excited to please his master, got busy right away and was very productive. God blessed his diligence with a ten-fold increase! Another servant was also industrious, and God blessed his efforts with a five-fold increase. Then there was one servant who did nothing with his lord's money.

On a day that no one expected, the nobleman returned from his journey and required an accounting as to their stewardship. The first servant came quickly, excited to announce that he had grown the one pound he had been given into ten pounds. He then heard the words from his master that were music to his ears and delight to his soul: "...Well, thou good servant: because thou hast been faithful in a very little, have thou authority over ten cities" (Luke 19:17).

The steward who increased his master's wealth five-fold approached, and his master likewise praised him: "...Be thou also over five cities" (Luke 19:19).

But the servant who had failed to put his resources to work was harshly condemned. His master called him wicked and took the one pound away from him and gave it to the servant who had gained ten pounds.

Our Lord Jesus Christ has gone to prepare a place for us. We do not know the day or the hour of His return. He has entrusted us with resources—physical, spiritual, and financial—and He expects us to use them to build His kingdom (not ours) while He is away.

The faithful servants in this parable increased the value of their master's estate. Likewise, as faithful stewards, we are to "further the kingdom of God," investing the resources God has given us in eternal riches.

> *Lay not up for yourselves treasures upon earth, where moth and rust doth corrupt, and where thieves break through and steal: But lay up for yourselves treasures in heaven, where neither moth nor rust doth corrupt, and where thieves do not break through nor steal: For where your treasure is, there will your heart be also.*
> —MATTHEW 6:19–21

Putting money to work wisely

What we have left after giving to the Lord is what we need to use to *occupy*. God expects us to provide for our families, enjoy the good things He has given us, and wisely prepare for the future. While the things of the world—houses, cars, clothing, and furniture—are temporary and will one day vanish, they are not evil in and of themselves.

Many financial struggles and problems can be averted if we would learn to save. Proverbs 21:20 says, "There is treasure to be desired and oil in the dwelling of wise, but a foolish man spendeth it up." If you spend every cent you make, you will have nothing left for "treasure" and "oil"—

economic commodities in Bible times. In fact, Solomon says we are being foolish if we spend it all.

It is good and right to pay all of your bills, but you should also pay yourself. Saving money is largely out of style in our day, but though it is difficult, it is not impossible. In fact, it is an integral part of occupying until the Lord returns. Life happens fast, and if we are not careful we will be tempted to "live in the moment" and spend money that we should be saving.

We will look at the importance of saving later in more detail, but for now remember that as long as we live in a fallen world, there will be problems, emergencies, unforeseen expenses, and illnesses that will require money. If we have not saved, we must then do without, beg for help from others, or go into debt. All of these options can generally be avoided by saving in the present.

Putting It into Practice

Can you confidently say that today you are living as the manager of God's resources and yielding to His ownership? _____

_____

If not, what do you believe is your greatest obstacle?_____

_____

_____

_____

Realizing that God has purchased you and owns you, your family, and your career, how should you handle the burdens in every aspect of your life?_____

_____

_____

_____

Looking through the lens of Scripture, how do you feel God would have you occupy until He comes?

_____

_____

_____

Assignment: Resolve to begin each day—before you get sidetracked or derailed—in prayer. Acknowledge God's ownership of everything in your life and give thanks for all that you have. God is good and He is sovereign. His ways are better than our ways!

Chapter Four
Eternal Thinking Today

Among the many distractions and obstacles that get in our way of biblical occupying, I believe the biggest culprit may be our lack of eternal thinking. It is all too easy to become "occupied" with the everyday cares of life. The concerns of daily living—safety, health, work, family, our rights as citizens, the politics of our land—are focused on temporal thinking.

Jesus warned us about this danger in Mark 4:18–19, "And these are they which are sown among thorns; such as hear the word, And the cares of this world, and the deceitfulness of riches, and the lusts of other things entering in, choke the word, and it becometh unfruitful."

There's an old saying that declares, "Youth is wasted on the young." As we get older we often wish we had the same level of energy, health and strength that we once enjoyed… while still knowing what we have learned in the passing years. It is also true that too often "Time is wasted on the temporal." How much of our lives are spent on things that are eternal, and how much is spent on things that will soon vanish away? What would happen if we consciously and deliberately lived each day with a focus on the eternal?

We live surrounded by people who are living for the moment. It's become common for someone about to do something crazy to say "YOLO"—you only live once. As Christians, however, we know that this isn't true. After this life is eternity. Everyone will live forever—either in Heaven or Hell. The "get all you can" mentality often infects Christian thinking and draws us toward the temporal. John issued a stern warning about this: "Love not the world, neither the things that are in the world. If any man love the world, the love of the Father is not in him. For all that is in the world, the lust of the flesh, and the lust of the eyes, and the pride of life, is not of the Father, but is of the world. And the world passeth away, and the lust thereof: but he that doeth the will of God abideth forever" (1 John 2:15–17).

If we let ourselves get caught up in chasing all that life has to offer, we easily lose sight of eternity. If we lose sight of eternity, we lose the urgency to use every resource and make it count for the cause of Christ. Suppose at your next doctor's appointment you were told you had just two weeks to live. What would you do differently? What would you stop doing? What would you start doing? How would you spend the time you had left?

The reality is that none of us knows how long we will live. There may be decades left, or there may only be hours. What would matter most to you if these were your last days on earth? Are you spending your days now on what would matter most then? If not, you need to make some changes. We should pray with the psalmist, "So teach us to number our days, that we may apply our hearts unto wisdom" (Psalm 90:12).

One night in the summer, as I was driving along a country road in North Carolina, I witnessed something I've not seen in the dry, high desert region of Southern California where I'm from. It had rained that afternoon, and as I was driving in the dark, I saw what looked like strange clouds rising up from the ground. It took me a few moments to realize what I was seeing. Although it was night, the pavement was still hot. The little wisps rising and then quickly disappearing in front of me were vapor! I was reminded of James 4:14 which tells us, "For what is your life? It is even a vapour, that appeareth for a little time, and then vanisheth away."

If we live thinking of eternity, we live with the awareness that eternity may arrive sooner than we think. Indeed, our lives are short—like a vanishing vapor. Every day in which we find ourselves with breath is an opportunity to share the truth of the gospel with another soul and transfer what we value here to our real and indescribable home with the Lord.

With the sobering reality that our lives are indeed short, why not live with that sense of urgency today? *Now*— not after a terminal diagnosis—is the time to be eternally minded. *Today* is the day to honor the Lord and further the kingdom.

We will give an account

As managers of our lives rather than owners, we will one day give an account to Jesus Christ who redeemed us by His blood. Satan, the father of lies, does his best to distract us from the reality of eternity. He does not want us to focus on the judgment seat of Christ. Our eternal security was settled at the cross, but we will be held responsible for what we do on earth with the time, opportunities, money, and gifts entrusted to us. Paul described this solemn day when we will give an account:

> *Now if any man build upon this foundation gold, silver, precious stones, wood, hay, stubble; Every man's work shall be made manifest: for the day shall declare it, because it shall be revealed by fire; and the fire shall try every man's work of what sort it is. If any man's work abide which he hath built thereupon, he shall receive a reward. If any man's work shall be burned, he shall suffer loss: but he himself shall be saved; yet so as by fire.*
> —1 CORINTHIANS 3:12–15

In the workplace, employees have managers and supervisors who hold them accountable for their responsibilities at work. Employees often handle company money, merchandise, and equipment. There are consequences for negligence just as there are rewards for diligence. If those in authority on earth hold us accountable, how much more will our Heavenly Father do the same?

I love the words of the Hymn "Turn Your Eyes upon Jesus" by Helen H. Lemmel:

> Turn your eyes upon Jesus,
> Look full in His wonderful face,

And the things of earth will grow strangely dim,
In the light of His glory and grace.

If we look to Jesus and focus on the moment when we will see Him face to face, if we consider eternity and the moment we stand before Him to give an account, it will change our lives. The temporal things of earth fade in comparison to the glory of the eternity that waits—and we need to live every day with eternity in view.

For which cause we faint not; but though our outward man perish, yet the inward man is renewed day by day. For our light affliction, which is but for a moment, worketh for us a far more exceeding and eternal weight of glory; While we look not at the things which are seen, but at the things which are not seen: for the things which are seen are temporal; but the things which are not seen are eternal.—2 Corinthians 4:16–18

Chapter Five
Treasures and Rewards

I da Wood first arrived in New York in 1857—a nineteen-year-old young woman determined she would become somebody. Listening to gossip and studying the society pages, she learned of a businessman and politician, Benjamin Wood. Soliciting Mr. Wood, who owned the *Daily News,* in a flattering letter, she won his heart and, eventually, his hand.

Ida hoarded money during their marriage. She even demanded half of her husband's winnings when he gambled but insisted he absorb all his losses himself. After the death of her husband, Ida sold the *Daily News* and moved into a rented room at the Herald Square Hotel where she lived as a recluse, frugally pinching pennies for the next twenty-four years.

In 1931, she was declared incompetent after her hotel room was discovered to be filled with filth and clutter. Among the piles of yellowed newspapers, cracker boxes, balls of used string, stacks of old wrapping paper, and several trunks, was an old shoe box which had $247,200 in cash, mostly in $1,000 and $5,000 bills (which were still in circulation at the time). In the pocket of the gown Ida was wearing there was $500,000 in $10,000 bills.

Among Ida's possessions was a $40,000 diamond necklace; bolts of the finest lace from Ireland, Venice, and Spain; necklaces, watches, bracelets, tiaras, and other gem-encrusted pieces; gold certificates dating back to the 1860s; and even an 1867 letter from Charles Dickens to Benjamin Wood.[1] But when she died on March 12, 1932, Ida Wood left this world and all the treasures that she had lived her entire life gaining.

Most of the verses in the Bible that deal with money are directed toward our hearts. God knows how we are drawn to money, riches, and possessions. He loves us too much not to warn us about the destruction and death that come from loving and trusting money. These warnings are not because He does not want us to have good things, but

---

1   Karen Abbott, "Everything Was Fake but Her Wealth" (Smithsonian. com, January 23, 2013), http://www.smithsonianmag.com/history/ everything-was-fake-but-her-wealth-4621153/?no-ist.

because He wants us to love real treasure, treasure we will be able to enjoy forever!

Literal, not metaphorical

Let's look carefully at the words of our Saviour in Matthew 6:19–21: "Lay not up for yourselves treasures upon earth, where moth and rust doth corrupt, and where thieves break through and steal: But lay up for yourselves treasures in heaven, where neither moth nor rust doth corrupt, and where thieves do not break through nor steal: For where your treasure is, there will your heart be also."

It is easy to read this passage of Scripture and think of it as metaphorical—an encouragement to good intentions. But this passage is much more than that. We can all relate to finding that things we enjoy don't last as long as we anticipated. Maybe the car gets a scratch in the parking lot or the dog chews the new sofa. Perhaps the brand new phone drops and shatters. Worse, perhaps someone breaks into our home and steals our valuable or sentimental possessions. The destruction or loss of things is a natural part of temporal possessions. By definition they don't last.

When Jesus talked about laying up "treasure in heaven" He was speaking of something real and precious. The word *treasure* in the Greek is *thesauros*. It is the same word we find in Matthew 2:11 when the wise men "opened their treasures" and presented them unto baby Jesus. These were real treasures: gold, frankincense, and myrrh—presents for the newborn King.

The greatest treasure in Heaven is Jesus Christ, our Saviour and Redeemer. We could spend all eternity doing nothing but gazing at His glory in worship and praise. It is not the streets of gold or the gates made of pearl that we will love; it is the Lamb of God. Yet during our lives on earth Christ encourages us not only to know the difference between worldly treasure and real, heavenly treasure, but to store up this eternal treasure for ourselves right now.

Randy Alcorn wrote, "Christ offers us the incredible opportunity to trade temporary goods and currency for eternal rewards. By putting our money and possessions in his treasury while we're still on earth, we assure ourselves of eternal rewards beyond comprehension."[2]

Self-interest, not selfishness

Jesus tells us to lay up these treasures in Heaven "for yourselves." This may seem to be an unusual instruction. Normally we are taught to put others first, to deny

2   Randy Alcorn, *Money, Possessions and Eternity* (Eternal Perspective Ministries, 2003), 96.

ourselves, that "the first shall be last, and the last first." Christ's instruction, however, is not at all an appeal to selfishness, but rather to self-interest. Christ is saying that the only way to keep what we treasure is to give it to Him. He offers a return on our investment that not only increases but is guaranteed, and not just for our lifetime but for all eternity—where it matters most.

When we give money to the Lord's work with the right heart, God literally sets that aside as treasure for us in Heaven. Why would we then want to hold tightly to the things that we cannot take with us? Why would we forfeit eternal treasure by clinging tightly to what we have? Solomon reminds us: "…and there is that withholdeth more than is meet, but it tendeth to poverty" (Proverbs 11:24). When we value eternal treasure, we will find it much easier to rightly handle our money here on earth.

Rewards

We learn the concept of rewards at a young age. Whether it was an ice cream cone after a ball game or a few dollars from our parents after we mowed the yard, it was a good thing to receive a reward. You probably noticed, however, that those rewards didn't last very long. The ice cream tasted good, but it was quickly eaten. The money may have purchased a toy, book, or game, but it also went away fast. These temporary rewards were worth having, but they didn't produce anything lasting.

As adults, we aspire toward different rewards. Maybe there is a bonus for meeting a production or sales goal at work. Perhaps there's an all-expenses-paid trip to a vacation spot. Although these rewards go far beyond an ice cream or a few dollars, there is still a sense that it doesn't last long. Does that mean it is foolish to try to get them? Are we selfish if we strive to win a game or make a sale? No. It is part of the way God designed us that we seek to better ourselves and receive rewards.

This principle applies to heavenly rewards as well. The Bible has a lot to say about these, yet often our focus is so earthly that we aren't very excited about heavenly rewards. (As a side note, let me point out that Heaven itself is not a reward—it is a gift. Our eternal salvation has nothing to do with our performance. It is all about what Jesus did for us. Ephesians 2:8–9 plainly says, "For by grace are ye saved through faith; and that not of yourselves: it is the gift of God: Not of works, lest any man should boast.")

Let's go back to the ice cream. What if you had an ice cream that you would eat and eat, and you just kept eating and it would never run out? Or what if the vacation in Hawaii never ended? Now that would be something to get excited about!

Rewards are given based on what we do for Christ, and Christ offers us many incentives—including tangible rewards and the opportunity to rule and reign with Him during the Millennial Kingdom. Though God's rewards are eternal and never end, many Christians view them without excitement. Why is that? Perhaps we are missing something important about God's promises regarding rewards.

We live in an age of instant gratification where we want good things right now. We don't like to wait. We even get frustrated when a smart phone takes more than ten seconds to open an app! (Oh, how far we've come.) When we learn of earning eternal rewards, it's easy to think, "But that's when I die, and that could be decades from now." And so we turn our focus instead toward the immediate opportunities of this life. It is as if we opt for ice cream when we could have Hawaii.

God wants us to be patient. Paul wrote, "But if we hope for that we see not, then do we with patience wait for it" (Romans 8:25). When we use our treasures on earth wisely for eternal things, we will receive eternal rewards at the Judgment Seat of Christ. "If any man's work abide which he hath built thereupon, he shall receive a reward" (1 Corinthians 3:14). Now that's something to work toward and wait for!

Putting It into Practice

Does the way you spend your time and money show a focus on eternity or on temporal things? _____

_____

_____

What is one thing you could do today with an eye toward eternal rewards? _____

_____

_____

What could you change in your life to increase your eternal impact? _____

_____

_____

Chapter Six
Financial Struggles

For my thoughts are not your thoughts, neither are your ways my ways, saith the Lord.—Isaiah 55:8

We will not get through life without trouble. And some of these troubles may very well come in the form of financial difficulties. Following God's principles for managing our money and keeping an eternal perspective does not negate the fact that we still live in a fallen world and face difficulties of every sort—including financial difficulties.

We can have a secure job, stay free of debt, and have money saved in the bank, yet still experience some form of financial hardship. Even with the most diligent planning and care, we are likely to experience financial needs. (As an example, many people today find themselves needing to help their parents with medical expenses in the later years of their lives. This can bring an added burden to our finances.) But, like every other burden in our lives, financial struggles can work to draw us closer to the Lord and to build our faith.

There are two basic categories of financial struggles—those we inflict upon ourselves and those over which we have no control at all. In either case, once we are experiencing the struggles, the answer is the same—trusting God. Sometimes this trust is expressed by realigning our use of money with God's principles. Sometimes it's expressed simply by holding to the promises of God.

Let's take a brief look at both types of financial struggle.

Father-Filtered Tests

Everything that comes into our lives—good or bad—can only reach us if God allows it. In other words, it is filtered through the hands of our loving Heavenly Father.

Any hardship we experience does not catch God by surprise. He intends rather that the trials He allows in our lives would draw us closer to Him and increase our trust in

Him. In fact, our greatest spiritual need after salvation is to depend completely on God and not on ourselves. Trials are excellent opportunities to grow in faith!

Several men of God have wisely said, "Don't let a trial go to waste!" What on earth do they mean? They mean that God has a purpose in what happens to us. The Apostle Peter reminds us, "Wherein ye greatly rejoice, though now for a season, if need be, ye are in heaviness through manifold temptations: That the trial of your faith, being much more precious than of gold that perisheth, though it be tried with fire, might be found unto praise and honour and glory at the appearing of Jesus Christ" (1 Peter 1:6–7).

I've certainly seen God use financial struggles in my own life to help me learn to trust Him more. In December of 1998, I left the security of a manager's salary to pursue self-employment in the financial services industry. The first few months went very well, and my wife and I rejoiced in God's provision. Then we hit a dry spell. Despite my very best efforts, we had no income for nearly three months. We even found ourselves facing the potential loss of our home. Needless to say, we were shaken.

Then, seemingly out of nowhere I received a call from a company that I had applied for a job with several years earlier. They were now interested in hiring me. So with renewed energy and vigor I made the two-hour drive to their headquarters several times for several interviews. (We really needed the money!) The interviews went well, and I was offered a job with a generous salary, a company car, and an expense account. It was a golden opportunity, which would definitely solve our financial problems. There was only one concern—I would have to move to be closer to my assigned territory of Laguna Beach, California. That was a problem for me because I knew that God had brought my family to Lancaster Baptist Church for a reason, and in the three years we had been attending, we had already witnessed the great things God was doing through that ministry and in our own lives.

I was in a bind. We had an immediate need of income, and there was an offer on the table that would make all my financial cares go away. Additionally, there was enormous pressure to take this offer, especially as I didn't have another visible direction to take. Yet, as I sought godly counsel, I came to realize that while there are other good churches, we were supposed to be where we were. With no Plan B, I made the hardest phone call I've ever had to make and told the company I was declining the offer.

In the world's eyes, that was a foolish decision. My pastor and church family were praying for us, and the very next month God provided for my financial services business above and beyond what I could ask or think! He provided income to meet our needs, pay the bills, and keep the house.

I don't have to tell you that our faith was strengthened during that trial. The job offer that appeared to be an answer to prayer was really a test—a trial that now is more precious to us than gold. We learned then, and continue to acknowledge today, that we are completely dependent on God, even (or perhaps especially) during times when we have no answers and do not understand what God is doing.

God knows our tomorrows, and He knows exactly what He wants to accomplish through the trials He allows in our lives. When we respond in faith during a trial and trust the Lord, we grow in patience and experience, and our faith is strengthened, preparing us for greater works God has in store for us. Ephesians 3:20–21 reminds us that in every circumstance God can work beyond our wildest dreams: "Now unto him that is able to do exceeding abundantly above all that we ask or think, according to the power that worketh in us, Unto him be glory in the church by Christ Jesus throughout all ages, world without end. Amen."

Self-Inflicted Pain

Not all of our financial struggles are trials which we had no ability to prevent. Some are simply the natural consequences of decisions that we make. What we do or do not do with money can create struggles and hardships in our marriages and even our walk with the Lord. God often allows us to suffer the consequences of bad choices so that we learn from our mistakes and stop repeating them.

Galatians 6:7 says, "Be not deceived; God is not mocked: for whatsoever a man soweth, that shall he also reap." Sometimes our financial problems relate to this simple law of sowing and reaping. If we sow in debt, we reap in burdens.

For instance, you cannot go out and buy a new wide screen television on credit and then expect God to provide the money to make the payments each month. A debt has been sown, a burden has been reaped, and there is a price to pay. We cannot put God "on the hook" and try to obligate Him to make it all better. When we suffer from self-inflicted financial problems, we are wise to remember that the same thinking that brought on the problem cannot be the same thinking to get us out.

When we discover that our financial problems are self-inflicted, we need to confess the sins (perhaps covetousness, poor stewardship, etc.) that brought us to that point and ask the Lord to help us change our practices. We need to align our beliefs of money, spending, and debt with God's Word.

Even then, there likely will not be an easy way out. The world sells the quick solution—the debt consolidation loan, the home equity loan—but those do not solve the problem and often make things worse. Part of the desirable outcome of a self-inflicted financial struggle is learning from the painful experience and being honest with ourselves about the thinking process that led to the mess we are in. The ultimate desirable outcome is learning to grow in our trust for God as we obey His ways.

Understand God's Promises

Whenever you are in a time of financial difficulty, beware of "solutions" that diminish your eternal perspective. The last thing you want to do is compound one mistake by making additional mistakes! During a financial struggle there is the temptation to rationalize that if you gave less to the Lord temporarily, there would be extra money to help you out of the struggle. Sometimes the devil tempts us with suggestions such as, "If you worked a couple of Sundays you could take that money and get out of this mess." God's will is never accomplished by going against His Word. Even if we are in trouble of our own making, God does not abandon us. When He allows us to suffer consequences it is for our own good.

Instead of insisting on going our own way, which is often what got us into trouble in the first place, God wants us to surrender our will to His. He will work with surrendered hearts, but if we are self-reliant we leave no room for God to do the work He desires in our lives. His promises require our trust and action, so that He can receive the glory instead of us.

This is what the Bible means when it says, "Trust in the Lord with all thine heart; and lean not unto thine own understanding. In all thy ways acknowledge him, and he shall direct thy paths" (Proverbs 3:5–6). Trust is required because what God tells us to do flies in the face of human wisdom. God's promises for those facing financial difficulties are centered on giving. As we saw in Chapter 3, our trust in God and obedience in our finances are connected in Proverbs 3. Just a few verses after the admonition to trust, we read, "Honour the Lord with thy substance, and with the firstfruits of all thine increase: So shall thy barns be filled with plenty, and thy presses shall burst out with new wine" (Proverbs 3:9–10).

This seems like a paradox. When we don't have enough money, we think we should hoard, but God says to give. When we put Him first, He responds. God's ways are not our ways, but they are the right ways. Jesus said, "Give, and it shall be given unto you; good measure, pressed down, and shaken together, and running over, shall men give into your bosom. For with the same measure that ye mete withal it shall be measured to you again" (Luke 6:38).

If you tell someone you are in a financial pinch and you have decided to start giving, they will probably think you are crazy. However, God receives glory when He does what is impossible for men. We are not following man's principles but God's. Proverbs 11:24–25 says, "There is that scattereth, and yet increaseth; and there is that withholdeth more than is meet, but it tendeth to poverty. The liberal soul shall be made fat: and he that watereth shall be watered also himself." Those who give, increase. Those who hold back, lose. It is the opposite of what man thinks, but it is true.

Chapter Seven
Avoiding Materialism's Destructive Pull

We live in a materialistic world that is always telling us we need more. More money. More recognition. More possessions. More…of everything.

Furthermore, our society promises that with "just a little more" we'll be happy. For instance, there are…

- Over 50,000 restaurants in just New York City.
- One hundred choices of lipstick to choose from at Nordstrom.
- Over 100,000 products to choose from at Wal-Mart.
- Approximately 250 different cereals to choose from in the grocery store. (This is my favorite aisle of the store!)

- An average of $27,000 is spent on a wedding, according to Bride's Magazine.

Yet at the same time:

- Arguing over money was a contributing factor in over 80 percent of divorces among young people.
- Each year there are more filings for bankruptcy than for new business licenses.

The world measures people by what they have accumulated. "More" has become the mantra of our culture. But more can never satisfy.

Although, as Christians, we may recognize the fallacy of putting our trust in more, we are not immune to the subtle pull of materialism. To guard our hearts against the destructive pull of materialism we need to identify the symptoms.

Materialism Revealed

Hosea 13:6 reveals what often happens in our hearts when we begin to accumulate *more*: "According to their pasture, so were they filled; they were filled, and their heart was exalted; therefore have they forgotten me."

The Israelites in Hosea's day were on a roller coaster. God would bless them, their hearts would be lifted up and consequently turned away from God. Then God would chasten them, allowing suffering. They would repent, turn to the Lord, and He would bless them. Then they would repeat the cycle—loving the blessings of God so they would turn from the Lord and go into idolatry again.

This cycle is similar to where we are in the United States right now. America is so prosperous that even the poorest people in our country are far better off than middle class people in many countries. And yet, as a nation we have turned from the Lord and are in love with prosperity.

From the pattern of the Israelites, notice two sure signals that we are falling prey to materialism's destructive pull.

Finding fulfillment in anything or anyone in place of God

God delivered the Children of Israel out of bondage in Egypt in a massive display of power. The ten plagues were more than just judgments on Egypt—they were directly aimed at the things Egyptians worshiped, proving that God was greater than the gods of the Egyptians. Yet not long after, when Moses went up on the mountain to get the law from God, Aaron made a golden calf for the people to worship. They wanted something tangible to worship.

I don't know any American Christians who set up physical idols to worship. But when we seek our fulfillment in money, possessions, status, or relationships, we're just as surely in the grip of idolatry as the Israelites were.

God wants and deserves our whole hearts. But the world tells us if we just had this toy or that job we would have happiness, contentment, and peace. And so we set our hearts on the toy or the job and, in the process, forget God and the priorities He has given us. To satisfy the pull of *more*, we work longer hours, neglecting our children and our church. We damage our families and impede our spiritual growth. Are there legitimate circumstances when a person must work long hours just to provide for their family? Absolutely. The question is not so much *what* we are doing, but rather *why* we are doing it. What is the motive for our actions?

A Christian may work longer hours away from his family, perhaps having to work on Sundays instead of going to church, robbing him of time to worship the Lord and impeding his spiritual growth. There are times when long hours of work are needed, but if we have our hearts set on *more* we are headed for trouble. The question is not so much *what* we are doing, but rather *why* we are doing it. What is the motive for our actions? If it is because our heart is set on more—if we are seeking fulfillment in anything or anyone other than God—we're headed for trouble.

The Bible gives us another sad account of a time when God's children found fulfillment in prosperity rather than in Him. Deuteronomy 32:15 says, "*But Jeshurun* [Israel] *waxed fat, and kicked: thou art waxen fat, thou art grown thick, thou art covered with fatness; then he forsook God which made him, and lightly esteemed the Rock of his salvation.*" It seems incredible that anyone could believe that something else could be better than God. Incredible, that is, when we look at other people's lives. Yet, if we are not careful, that is exactly what can eventually take place in our own hearts and lives.

Trusting in money rather than God

Money is not a bad thing. God expects us to provide for the needs of our families. We need money to cover everything from mortgages to medical bills, from electricity to education, from bacon to braces! We have to write budgets, plan for the future, pay close attention to our bank account balances, discern needs from wants, and deal with unexpected problems. All too often, without even realizing it, a Christian can shift his focus and trust away from God and toward money. You can identify this subtle shift if you start hearing yourself say phrases like, "I just don't see how we can give this week."

If we were asked, "Do you trust your dollars or do you trust God?" most Christians would quickly answer, "God, of course." Yet our actions don't always match that answer. We are likely to make the wrong choices when we let worry and stress influence our financial decisions. Our flesh gravitates toward what we can see and touch. The devil is quick to tempt with worrisome thoughts like, "If you tithe, how are you going to pay your bills?" or "How are you going to have enough to buy Christmas gifts?" While the devil may be good at questioning, God is perfect in His *telling*! Consider these principles:

- **God alone provides our source of income:** "But thou shalt remember the LORD thy God: for it is he that giveth thee power to get wealth…" (Deuteronomy 8:18).

- **Riches are uncertain:** "He that trusteth in his riches shall fall: but the righteous shall flourish as a branch" (Proverbs 11:28).

- **Riches comes from God:** "Charge them that are rich in this world, that they be not highminded, nor trust in uncertain riches, but in the living

God, who giveth us richly all things to enjoy"
(1 Timothy 6:17).

In light of these principles, materialism is pretty
shallow, isn't it?

We've seen two revealing signs of materialism's pull
in our lives. But it gets worse! Let's now look at the results
of materialism.

Materialism Realized

Satan's snares do not start off with pain and heartbreak. (If
they did, people wouldn't sin.) Instead he starts us with
pleasure and with what seems to be good results. It is only
later that the trouble sets in. Materialism works that same
way. James 1:15 says, "Then when lust hath conceived, it
bringeth forth sin: and sin, when it is finished, bringeth
forth death."

Notice some of the consequences that follow the sin
of materialism:

Idolatry

Idolatry is putting things in the place of God instead of
putting Him first. Colossians 3:5 makes a direct correlation
between covetousness (the desire for more) and idolatry:

"Mortify therefore your members which are upon the earth; fornication, uncleanness, inordinate affection, evil concupiscence, and **covetousness, which is idolatry**."

The things that we make our idols are not always wrong things, they are just things that take our time, affection, money, and interest away from God. So many things in our world are calling for our attention and time. According to recent studies, the average American who uses social media spends 3.6 hours every day socializing online.[1] When we dedicate this kind of time to entertainment or amusement, we are on the slippery slope toward idolatry. We give our time to who or what we value. Thus, time is one of the best gauges of our hearts.

Self-Destruction

Paul uses strong and graphic terms to describe those who desire riches: "But they that *will be rich* fall into temptation and a snare, and into many foolish and hurtful lusts, which drown men in destruction and perdition. For the love of money is the root of all evil: which while some coveted

---

1   "Socialogue: The Most Common Butterfly on Earth Is the Social Butterfly" (Ipsos Research Comapany, January 8, 2013), http://ipsos-na.com/news-polls/pressrelease.aspx?id=5954.

after, they have erred from the faith, and pierced themselves through with many sorrows" (1 Timothy 6:9–10).

The phrase "will be rich" emphasizes that this passage is not just talking about wealth itself. (Remember, even Americans who are below poverty level are wealthier than most other people in the world.) It is talking about a consuming desire for wealth—a person who focuses his will power on amassing riches.

What happens to people who *will* be rich? They fall into temptation and a snare (a trap or noose) and into many foolish and hurtful lusts. These foolish and hurtful lusts then drown men in destruction and perdition. When someone drowns, their lungs are filled with water so there is no room for air. As a result, they die. Similarly, riches fill our hearts so there is no room for God.

If that were not caution enough, Paul continues. Those who love riches err from the faith and pierce themselves with many sorrows. This sounds like something reasonable people should desire with all their might to avoid!

Remember, Paul wrote this to Timothy regarding *Christians*. Salvation does not exempt us from the love of money. As Christians, we must be vigilant against this downward spiral that destroys lives, families, testimonies and churches.

Loss of opportunity

As God's children, we have certainly been given much more than we deserve. As we saw in chapter 3, God calls us to be faithful stewards of everything with which we have been entrusted. This doesn't only apply to our money, but to every resource God has given us—including our health, family, influence, and even the gospel itself.

With these gifts, God has given us another valuable gift. It's called "today," and we are to use it wisely. We do not know that God will give us the gift of "tomorrow."

Today is the day of opportunity. *Today* is the day to give and further the cause of Christ! Materialism causes us to lose opportunities for the eternal because we are worrying over money and hesitant in giving. It leads us to squander our resources by buying things that are unnecessary and frivolous.

God is very interested with how you live your life and what you do with what He entrusts to you during your life here on Earth. When we stand before the Lord, we will be required to give an account of everything we have done. If we have trusted Christ as our Saviour, our eternal destiny is settled, so this time of accounting is not about whether or not we will enter Heaven. Rather, this time is about what we have done with the opportunities and resources God gave to us.

First Corinthians 3:12–14 describes this time: "Now if any man build upon this foundation gold, silver, precious stones, wood, hay, stubble; Every man's work shall be made manifest: for the day shall declare it, because it shall be revealed by fire; and the fire shall try every man's work of what sort it is. If any man's work abide which he hath built thereupon, he shall receive a reward."

When we stand before Christ to give an account, we will not have second chances. In the presence of His holiness we will be all too aware of our own lost opportunities during our lives.

When our works are tried with fire, the things in this life that we worried about and stressed over are all going to be consumed and will be no more. However, everything that we gave to the Lord and trusted to Him will remain with us forever. As the missionary C.T. Studd wisely said, "Only one life 'twill soon be past, only what's done for Christ will last."

Materialism Repealed

As powerful as materialism is, we do not have to give in to it. If we are cautious and alert to its subtle temptation, we can overcome it. God has given us the power to have the victory—but we must stop and think.

In Jesus' parable of the Prodigal Son, we hear about the younger of two sons who selfishly and hurtfully demanded that his father give him his inheritance. Considering that inheritances are generally distributed upon the death of a parent and this young man's father was very much alive, his request was not only unreasonable but selfish as well.

The father obliged his son and sadly handed over his "share" of the estate. Soon after, this young man went far from home and did everything his heart desired. The Bible states that he "…wasted his substance with riotous living" (Luke 15:13). The Greek word for *riotous* means "dissolutely, lacking moral restraint; indulging in sensual pleasures or vices."

Of course this behavior (and his pleasure in it) couldn't last longer than his money. When the money ran out, so did his friends and his fun. His situation soon became especially dire because of a great famine in the area, and eventually he found himself not only tending swine in hopes of earning some money, but desiring to eat what the pigs were eating—which is pretty bad for a young Jewish man!

One day, hungry and dissatisfied, he finally decided to stop and think. Luke 15:17 records, "And when he came to himself, he said, How many hired servants of my father's have bread enough and to spare, and I perish with hunger!" Sometimes it takes painful consequences to get our attention. Sometimes it takes being buried in debt for someone to realize that he is destroying himself and his family. Sometimes it takes a person who is addicted to alcohol or drugs getting into an auto accident or hurting someone before they "come to themselves."

If you believe that materialism even has a "tiny" hold (and there really is no such thing—it is always a big problem) in your heart or mind, stop and think. Be honest before the Lord and ask God, as David of old asked, "Search me, O God, and know my heart: try me, and know my thoughts: And see if there be any wicked way in me, and lead me in the way everlasting" (Psalm 139:23–24).

There is on old expression that says: "Sin will take you farther than you want to go, keep you longer than you want to stay, and cost you more than you want to pay." Perhaps nowhere is that more true than in the matter of materialism.

So what can you do to overcome materialism? You need a plan. A plan without action produces no positive change. The outcome of the prodigal son's thinking was a decision. He didn't just think about his misery—he made a plan to go to his father's house, and he went. He put his feet on the road and headed toward home.

Ask God for forgiveness

Just as he humbly returned to his father, we need to humbly return to our Father in Heaven and seek His forgiveness for our materialism. Remember that the battle against materialism, even though it involves physical possessions, is still a spiritual battle. It can only be fought and won with God's power.

Replace materialism with contentment

Many years ago Carnation Milk used a slogan to sell their product: "Our milk comes from contented cows." I don't know if their milk was any better than their competitors or not, but they were on to a great truth—being contented produces good results in every part of life. To the contrary, being discontented places us in grave danger of materialism.

A popular newspaper did a survey of forty-five-year-old people. The majority of those polled said that they would be happier if they could make another $8,000 to $10,000 a year. The reality, however, is that if they got that raise and were interviewed again a year later, they would still wish for another $10,000 more! More can never make us happy. That is a powerful lie from Satan. Look at what God has to say about contentment:

- Contentment is a **learned** state. Paul wrote: "Not that I speak in respect of want: for I have learned, in whatsoever state I am, therewith to be content" (Philippians 4:11). Paul wrote these words in an unsanitary dungeon, in the worst of physical conditions. Roman jailers were not known for their kind treatment of prisoners. Yet even in that state, Paul was content. This is not something he started out with. He had to learn it.

- Contentment is a **flexible** state. Paul continued: "I know both how to be abased, and I know how to abound: every where and in all things I am instructed both to be full and to be hungry, both to abound and to suffer need" (Philippians 4:12).

During World War II, Corrie ten Boom, along with her sister, Betsie, were placed in a German concentration camp because the ten Booms were rescuing Jews from the Gestapo. During their imprisonment, they were moved to a camp that was infested with fleas. Even the straw they were given to sleep on moved—because it was so full of fleas. As Corrie was complaining about the fleas one day, her sister challenged her to be thankful for them! "Betsie, there's no way even God can make me grateful for the fleas," Corrie responded. They had been studying 1 Thessalonians, and Betsie reminded Corrie, "The Bible says to give thanks in *all* circumstances; it doesn't say only in *pleasant* circumstances." And so Betsie stopped and gave thanks for the fleas. Not long after, the sisters learned that the fleas had actually protected them from the assaults of the German soldiers and allowed them to hold Bible studies without being interrupted!

Nothing happens to you by mistake. Trust God and be content in whatever state your life is in.

Putting It into Practice

Is there any area in my life, heart or thought process that is turning away from God? _____

_____

_____

Am I starting to trust in money more than God? _____

_____

_____

_____

Am I worrying over financial matters rather than trusting God? _____

_____

_____

Have I reduced or stopped giving to God because of financial pressure? _____

_____

_____

Chapter Eight
Harmony in the Home

By God's design, marriage is for life. Ephesians 5:31 says, "For this cause shall a man leave his father and mother, and shall be joined unto his wife, and they two shall be one flesh." A man and a woman come together and become one. Yet today divorce is rampant, and one of the leading causes of divorce is conflict over financial issues. Even couples who stay together are often bitterly divided over money issues.

Imagine you are on a date with the love of your life just weeks before your wedding. You are having a nice dinner together, the ambiance is just right, there's soft music playing, and then one of you asks the other, "So, what are your beliefs on how a credit card should be used?" The music suddenly comes to a screeching halt, and everyone who is close enough to hear leans in with interest. Not exactly romantic is it?

It's safe to say that most couples do not inquire too deeply into the area of financial beliefs. It is not fun, and it is certainly not romantic. The subject is usually avoided. Yet money tends to be one of the leading causes of disagreements, division, and divorce. While Christian couples may very well share the same spiritual beliefs, they often do not share the same financial beliefs. Frequently the impact of these varying beliefs does not surface for months or years into a marriage.

As I talk with couples regarding money issues, I've found that often they have not taken into account the impact of their upbringing on their views about money. Your spouse more than likely had different influences while growing up. Being born into a different family than yours, and likely a different community, state, or even country, they experienced different conditioning. As a result, they simply view money through a different lens—and that can lead to trouble, particularly when those differences are not understood and taken into account.

Perhaps while you were growing up you heard sayings like, "Money doesn't grow on trees, you know!" or "Eat all your supper. There are starving children in

Africa." If that was your upbringing, you probably have a more conservative attitude toward money. But let's say instead you grew up in a home where your parents gave you pretty much anything you wanted or asked for. In that case you may have a more casual approach. It is easy to see why conflict can arise between two people with varying backgrounds.

Based on our upbringing, we develop beliefs, thoughts, stories, attitudes, and assumptions about money that heavily influence the financial decisions we make throughout our lives. Most people adopt the same habits or disciplines (or the lack of them) toward money as their parents do. While early conditioning does not excuse unhealthy or destructive adult financial behavior, understanding how a person was brought up to view money helps understand the current beliefs and behavior patterns. For example, one spouse may have no interest in creating and maintaining a savings account. Perhaps he saw his parents try to save but failing because something always "came up" that caused them to spend whatever they had accumulated. As a result he doesn't see any point in trying to save money and may be resistant to the idea of starting a savings account.

Once we identify an unhealthy belief about money we can find Bible precepts and principles to correct that problem. For example, a person who does not want to save may be helped by the teaching of Proverbs 21:20, which says, "There is treasure to be desired and oil in the dwelling of the wise; but a foolish man spendeth it up."

Arguments over money have enormous power because, to us, what we believe about money from our upbringing is "normal," and having a spouse go against these beliefs seems destructive. This comes out even more when there is serious financial trouble. Money quickly becomes a very emotional issue. The devil uses these emotional conflicts to drive a wedge between husband and wife. Without open and loving communication, bitterness can spring up and lead to the ultimate destruction of a marriage and family.

Examining Influences

Here is an exercise that will help you, as a couple, to identify the source of the attitudes toward money that you brought into your marriage. Before you work through these questions together, take a moment to pray together that God will use this to build understanding and strengthen your relationship. Remember that this is not the place for blame—it is simply an identifying exercise to help build understanding. Each spouse should write their own answers to these questions and after finishing the exercise share their answers with the other.

1. What sayings about money did you hear while growing up?
2. What would you say your father's beliefs about money are or were?
3. What would you say your mother's beliefs about money are or were?
4. From the answers to questions three and four, identify which of those beliefs or sayings would be considered destructive and which ones are healthy. Write your appraisal of each belief next to that belief—a "D" for destructive and an "H" for healthy.
5. Do you think you have accepted or rejected those beliefs?
6. How do you believe this has influenced you today?

If each person has been transparent, this exercise will help couples have a better understanding of the financial influences which have impacted and conditioned them, and it will prepare you to work together to make things better.

My wife and I benefited greatly from this exercise. Prior to working through this together, we tried to avoid talking about money because we knew it would lead to disagreements. However, we knew we needed help, so we spent time in prayer and then went through the exercise. Answering these questions helped us understand each other better, but it also helped us understand ourselves. As we worked through our answers, I realized that I had developed some destructive beliefs about the way my wife handled money. I had wrongly believed that my wife was the spender and that "I, and I alone" was the saver. I was not correct in what I thought, so I set out to change. First I communicated that to her, and then I made a major change in the way we managed our family finances. She became much more involved, and it made things much better. My wife likewise recognized things from her past that were influencing her approach to money. She grew up in a household with no apparent financial struggles, and she was given the things that she wanted. After her parents divorced, however, her father began giving her more gifts and things, possibly because of his guilt. Her mother was not a saver, so that influenced her view of money as well. Recognizing the source of our attitudes toward money not only helped us make better financial decisions, but it strengthened our marriage by helping us understand each other.

A Price to Pay

Living according to destructive beliefs about money takes a toll not only on individuals but on families as well. These negative consequences can include lack of savings, decreased giving, an unwillingness or inability to help others, a lack of confidence, damaged relationships, and physical illness from stress and worry. So why do people pay this kind of price? Because they get something out of it. Here are some of the "gains" from destructive beliefs about money: control, blaming others, avoiding responsibility, self-righteousness, avoiding communication, and being a martyr. Even though these "gains" are destructive, people often cling tightly to their beliefs because of the emotional payoff.

The beliefs that we bring to marriage are powerful, but they are not set in stone. When we have identified a destructive belief, we can reject it and replace it with a biblical principle. We can choose to believe what is true and helpful instead of what is destructive. The keys to change are identifying the destructive belief (often we are unaware of the beliefs that actually drive our actions)and then making a conscious decision to replace that belief with a correct one.

Chapter Nine
A Biblical Approach to Money Management

The world is full of advice for managing money, but much of it makes things worse instead of better. The Bible, however, gives us many promises and principles that, when followed, will provide peace and joy in place of stress and fear. It is quite exciting to know that God has chosen us and equipped us to be His stewards of the resources He has graciously entrusted to us. We have all the resources of Heaven at our disposal to accomplish His will on earth. So let's look at what God says about managing our money.

Give to the Lord

The most important principle in the Bible regarding money is that we must always put God first. When you receive

income, which God has provided (Deuteronomy 8:18),
pay the Lord what is His before anything else. Give out of
a grateful heart, and trust Him to keep His promises to
provide for you. Unfortunately many Christians, when they
receive their income, pay their bills first and deal with the
things which are "screaming the loudest." Then, if there is
any money left over, they consider what they can give to the
Lord. If there is abundance one month, they may give more
and if a particular month is tight, they simply try to give
next month.

People who take this approach quickly get trapped
in a vicious cycle. The financial "light at the end of the
tunnel" always seems to be just out of reach. They take the
world's wisdom rather than God's wisdom, and suffer as
a result. When we truly trust God and pay Him first, our
faith is strengthened as we see Him provide. Remember,
God doesn't need our money—everything already belongs
to Him. Giving is necessary because we need the work that
God desires to do in and through us when we step out by
faith and put Him first.

God wants us to have something more important and
more valuable than money. Peter wrote, "That the trial of
your faith, being much more precious than of gold that
perisheth, though it be tried with fire, might be found

unto praise and honour and glory at the appearing of Jesus Christ" (1 Peter 1:7).

Obedience strengthens our faith, and it also brings praise, glory, and honor to God.

Pay yourself

We have looked at the verse before, but it bears repeating here. Proverbs 21:20 says, "There is treasure to be desired and oil in the dwelling of the wise; but a foolish man spendeth it up." It is rather difficult for a dwelling to have treasure and oil—which are very valuable commodities—unless the occupant saved over time. Unexpected expenses are part of life. Unless we have some money in reserve, they can quickly become major problems. In addition, wisdom sets aside money to help provide for future years when we may not be able to work.

The concept of saving is easy to understand, but it can be very difficult to practice. Most people do not put money aside for the future on a regular basis. Some of the reasons I've heard for not saving are: "The banks aren't paying any interest," "Saving is boring," and "I can't afford to save any money."

We need to recognize that the results of not saving are harmful and dangerous. Many people get deeply in debt because they have no funds to respond to emergencies. Even things that are not emergencies but must be replaced because of normal wear and tear—tires, clothing, and appliances—have to be paid for in some way. It is always better to save and have the means to pay for these needs when they come up.

Are you currently paying yourself on a regular basis? If so, do you have a set percentage? By determining a percentage of your income you are assuring consistency. Without a standard in saving (just as with giving) the result is usually "hit and miss." You save when you think about it and as long as there is extra money, or you don't save because something came up. The hit-and-miss approach creates not only frustration but also dismal results.

After you have determined your income and outflow (which we will cover later), commit a set monthly amount from your discretionary dollars and have it automatically transferred from your checking account to a savings account. Some people, depending on their level of discipline, find it helpful to have the savings account at a completely different bank to avoid the temptation to spend it as soon as a little money accumulates.

It is a good goal to set aside at least 10 percent of your income in savings. That may not be practical as you start your money management plan. Perhaps all you will be able to do at first is 5 percent. But whatever the amount, it is important to start with something. Saving is a habit and a discipline. The more you do it, the easier it becomes.

Purchase according to your needs

The Children of Israel needed food as they traveled to the Promised Land, and God provided manna for them. God gave clear instructions that they were to gather up enough manna for each person in their family to eat for one day— no more. Once a week, on the sixth day only, they were to gather up two days' worth of this heavenly food so that they would not have work on the Sabbath. Those with larger families gathered much, those with smaller families gathered less, but all were satisfied and there was nothing in excess, neither was there lacking.

The temptation of course was to gather extra "in case" there was no more manna to be found the next day. There even may have been opportunists who would gather up excess with the intention on selling their abundance to others, but this was not God's plan. If any man took more than what was instructed, thus disobeying and not trusting in God, his food spoiled—worms grew in it and it smelled horrible. In this exercise of faith, God was teaching His children to trust solely on Him, not the food which they could see and touch.

With the warehouse-type stores we have today, it is easy to purchase our groceries and household items needed for a week and perhaps even longer. No longer do we have to go out each day and get our food. Yet the principles God gave us still apply today. It is very easy, and tempting to "over buy," purchasing more than we need. Store management teams work hard to capture as many dollars from you as they can with "sales" and displays designed to capture your attention and create the desire for ownership.

This is where wise stewardship applies. Remember the words of Christ as He taught us to pray, "Give us this day our daily bread" (Matthew 6:11). This does not mean we should not plan for the future—it means we should not squander our resources on impulse purchases or wasteful items. We should be focused on our actual needs and be content as long as those are met.

Set a reasonable budget for groceries and clothing and household items, and then abide by it. It is helpful to sit down two or three times a year and review how much on average your family is spending in these categories and then compare these amounts to your written budget. (It can be an eye-opening exercise when you look at your bank statements and actually add up the dollars you are spending.) This allows for you to make adjustments if you are overspending and return to your previously agreed upon budget.

Some time ago my wife and I reviewed the amount we were spending on groceries, and my jaw dropped! For a time we had not closely monitored the amounts. When we looked back on our last three months of bank statements, we were shocked at what we found. On average, we were spending $200 per month over our budget. As a result of being more careful—not doing without necessities but being deliberate with our purchases—we were able to reallocate that $200 to more important areas.

Save for major purchases

Our culture screams, "You've got to have the newest and the best, and you've got to have it right now!" We are inundated with product commercials designed to create the desire of ownership. Companies spend billions of dollars every year to make us want what we don't have.

Before buying major items, we should first exercise self-control and prayerfully consider what is a "want" and what is a "need." There is nothing wrong with getting a "want" if God has provided the resources for it, but those should never come before our needs. With either a want or need, the importance of fighting the temptation to have it now cannot be over-emphasized.

My dad used to tell me, "What is worth having is worth saving for." That is really good advice, but we don't always want to hear it. Our flesh craves what we want right now! Jesus said, "For which of you, intending to build a tower, sitteth not down first, and counteth the cost, whether he have sufficient to finish it?"(Luke 14:28). Whether your "tower" is a home, a car, or an entertainment center, the principle is the same—can you pay for it today without getting yourself in the bondage of debt? If the answer to that question is "no," don't buy it.

A second benefit to saving for a purchase is that it takes time. During that time, the initial euphoria you felt for the item may fade, and you may choose to do something else with the money. Most of us have had the experience of getting something we just had to have only to find that as the novelty and newness wore off, we regretted spending the money. Often Americans are materially rich but cash poor because so many do not save.

Avoid making financial decisions on the assumption of future finances

The housing bubble in the United States during the early 2000s was largely the result of assumptions. Countless families purchased homes with an adjustable rate mortgage or with a balloon payment, and were assured that they could simply re-finance their loan within five years to avoid a higher payment. Since prices of homes had been rising and rising, the assumption was that they would continue to rise. Yet from the peak of the market, the average value of a home in the United States fell nearly 33 percent. Those who had mortgages depending on re-financing, found that they could not, as they owed more than the house was worth. As a result, a great number of homeowners lost their homes. It is dangerous to presume upon the future.

In 1990, the company I was working for was in the process of being purchased by a larger company. The "word" among the managers was that the new company paid their managers better and that we should expect a raise of about $500 a month. At the time, my young family needed a car to replace the two-seater truck I was driving. I reasoned that, even if my pay stayed the same, we could afford the monthly payment of a new car, so we took on that debt.

When the new company took over, my income did not go up. In fact, it did not even stay the same—it dropped by several hundred dollars per month! As you can imagine, that put quite a squeeze on an already tight budget. We had to make uncomfortable adjustments, including my wife taking a part-time job when we both preferred her to stay home with our one-year-old son. But because of my decision to act on the assumption of a raise, we had no other choice.

When any long-term financial commitment is made, we must recognize that the longer the time commitment is, the greater the risk is that there will be a change to your finances. It is advisable to keep a margin in your monthly budget, instead of bringing your spending and commitments up to the level of your income. For example, a prudent guideline for a home purchase is that the payment (principle, interest, taxes, and insurance) should be no more than one third of your monthly income. Even then, you should not go all the way up to that amount unless after paying God and yourself and covering your bills there will still be several hundred dollars left over. It is far better to buy "less" house and be able to pay for it than to be under constant pressure or lose your home.

Building margin into your finances allows you to respond to the inevitable changes in life and the unexpected expenses that arise without threatening your ability to make your house payment. Home buyers need to be cautious and wise, deciding before a home is chosen what the maximum monthly payment they will assume will be. It is easy to get caught up in the euphoria and romance of a beautiful house, which can lead to irrational compromises: "I know the payment would be higher than we want, but if we generated our own electricity and skipped one meal each day we can *totally* make this happen!"

Avoid debt on depreciating items

We can certainly learn from Scripture that God does not want His children to be in bondage. Proverbs 22:7 wisely warns, "The rich ruleth over the poor, and the borrower is servant to the lender."

No one wants to be a slave. No one dreams of the day when their choices are taken away and all their work is for the benefit of someone else. Yet because of the desire to "have it all and have it now," millions of consumers are going into slavery, one swipe of the credit card at a time. There are countless credit card holders making payments this month for last year's gasoline and last year's steak dinner. That is slavery.

I know that some people question going into debt for anything, even a home. However, the reality is that only a tiny fraction of the population can pay cash for a house. Here are some things to consider that make a mortgage different from other kinds of debt.

- A mortgage is debt, but it is a debt with an option. You can sell your home and repay the debt.

(Assuming you have purchased wisely and the price has increased, you may actually walk away with far more money than you started with—but you should not assume that is what will happen.)

- Many times borrowing money to buy a home will provide a lower overall cost than renting, especially with the tax advantage that goes to those who own their homes.

- The purchase of a home should not be considered a short-term undertaking. In the short-term, values can drop dramatically—as we witnessed during the real estate crash.

Most of the money people owe in the United States today is not for homes, but for other things—usually for things that are losing value every day. Financing something like that is not a wise decision, because by the time you finally pay it off, it may be worth nothing at all. Debt creates bondage, so it should be avoided as much as possible.

Have a simple, written, God-honoring spending plan

Budgets get a bad rap. I've never yet counseled someone who was excited about making one. Budgets are viewed often as being restrictive or binding, as something that takes the fun out of life. And though a budget is a good and important tool, it can be misused.

During the first couple of years of my marriage I wrongly used budgets to control rather than to help. I imposed a tight grocery budget of $75 a week (that included the purchase of diapers). I would check the store receipts after my wife went shopping to see that she stayed within the budget. If $85 was spent instead of $75, I would get upset. This is a good example of a bad example! I have long since repented, God has been merciful, and my wife did not kill me.

A budget is simply a written spending plan. When you and your spouse work on it together, agree on the finished plan, and follow it, you will find that a budget can be empowering. When you actually see where the money is going, you can discover opportunities to be more efficient with your income and make better progress toward family goals.

There is a "Cash Flow" exercise my wife and I do at least once a year, and recommend to those I counsel that they do the same.[1] You will need your last three

---

1   You can download a copy of the worksheet that I use at strivingtogether.com/downloads/worksheet.

months of bank and credit card statements (to determine monthly averages), amounts of your current monthly bills (mortgage, utilities, etc.), a sheet of paper or a blank spreadsheet on the computer, and some highlighter pens.

Take the sheet of paper (or open spreadsheet), and at the top left corner write your household's average monthly income—your "take home" amount, not the gross.

Below income, begin listing your "fixed" items. These are items that recur every month.

I recommend writing "tithe," "offering," and "missions" first, reminding us to put God first and trust Him to meet our needs with the remaining dollars.

Second, put savings—remember the importance of paying yourself.

Next, list your mortgage or rent, insurance(s), utilities, auto payment (if applicable), gasoline, school loans (if applicable), and so on. List everything that needs to be paid every month.

The next section is for "variable" items. This is where the bank and credit card statements come into play. Take a highlighter and begin highlighting categories of expenses, using a different colored highlighter for each category if possible. You're looking for items such as "dining out" (which includes coffee purchases and fast food), "personal care," "clothing," "entertainment," "travel," "groceries" (because this can vary in amounts and is controllable), "household items," "doctor visits," "child care," and "animal care"—to name a few. You may be surprised at how many different categories you actually spend money on!

Now add up the total dollars for all three months—one category at a time. Then divide that total by three to see your monthly "average" in each category. For example, a household may have spent $625 on groceries in March, $820 in April and $760 in May. The average monthly grocery expense is $735.

$$\$625 + \$820 + \$760 = \$2,205 \qquad \$2,205 \div 3 = \$735$$

If all consenting parties agree that this is a reasonable amount, this becomes the monthly grocery budget. On the other hand, if you are shocked to discover that what you are spending on groceries is far more than you thought, this is your opportunity to lower that amount and agree to stay with that new number.

As you complete this step for every "variable" item, you may indeed discover that far too many dollars are being spent in areas that can be cut back without causing any suffering in the family. When you have identified the current amounts of each category "flowing out" of your family's hands, you then can agree on reasonable new amounts and purpose together to maintain your new spending plan.

Chapter Ten

A Balance Between Managing for Today and Planning for Tomorrow

As adults we have plenty of responsibilities for today, among which are paying our bills and keeping our families alive by not forgetting to feed them and give them shelter! In the busyness of life it's easy to get near-sighted, addressing financial needs mainly as they come up without a long-term view in mind. This puts many families in a reactive mode versus a proactive mode.

Yes, we must manage the needs of the day, earning an income and working to stay within our budget. Yet we must also plan for tomorrow. The imbalances between the two are easy to see. Some say "*Carpe Diem!*" or "Live for today!"

and find that "tomorrow" comes sooner than they thought, leaving them ill-prepared.

Solomon cautions against this imbalanced approach to handling our money. In Proverbs 21:17, we learn that spending our resources in the pursuit of pleasure leads to poverty, "He that loveth pleasure shall be a poor man: he that loveth wine and oil shall not be rich."

Earlier we looked at the young man whom we know as the prodigal son in Luke 15. He is a perfect example of this problem. Once he received his inheritance prematurely, he did not lay out a prudent savings plan to last his lifetime. Instead, he thought only of the moment with no thought of the future. The Bible says, "And when he had spent all, there arose a mighty famine in that land; and he began to be in want." He didn't see that famine coming, and he found himself ill-prepared to face it. Likewise, many people today are not planning adequately for the future.

We also see wise counsel against the *opposite* of living only for today. Just as frivolous spending is dishonoring to God, so is hoarding—holding on to as much as possible—for fear of the future. I once sat down with a Christian retired couple who were living off their Social Security income. They had saved and invested over the years and accumulated well over $600,000. Choosing to eat mostly noodles and hot dogs, they resisted touching their savings for fear they would run out of money. While their diet is their prerogative, their money was doing neither earthly or eternal good. Solomon calls such action "a sore evil": "There is a sore evil which I have seen under the sun, namely, riches kept for the owners thereof to their hurt" (Ecclesiastes 5:13).

Another danger is that of presumption—assuming we know the future and willfully making financial decisions without seeking the guidance of God or recognizing our dependence upon God. James 4:13–15 cautions against this presumption: "Go to now, ye that say, To day or to morrow we will go into such a city, and continue there a year, and buy and sell, and get gain: Whereas ye know not what shall be on the morrow. For what is your life? It is even a vapour, that appeareth for a little time, and then vanisheth away. For that ye ought to say, If the Lord will, we shall live, and do this, or that."

How then do we strike the proper balance? I believe it begins with an understanding that instead of *two* time frames to consider—now and later in life—there are actually *three* very real time frames we are to prepare for—now, later in life, and our eternal life. Let's define these periods:

Now

This is the short term—today, tomorrow, next week, next month, the rest of the year. Now is the time to make intentional decisions which will surely impact our future life here, as well as in eternity.

Later in Life

This is the point in life when we are no longer working. Retirement as we know it today is relatively new. We do not read about retirement in Scripture, and it was only as recently as the nineteenth century in America that the first pension plan was created, followed by the Social Security program in 1935.

God designed man to labor. Man designed retirement and the concept of living in leisure and set the age of sixty-five as the standard. While I am not proposing that a man work until he takes his last breath, it is true that Christians should labor for the Lord all of our lives. If we are financially able to retire from the workforce, we should consider volunteering in ministry and serving the Lord. If, during the course of your working years, your health fails or you are injured or become disabled, how will the living expenses for you and your family be paid? This is the purpose for saving and investing for later in life. Proverbs 11:16 says, "A gracious woman retaineth honour: and strong men retain riches."

Eternal Life

We are clearly admonished in God's Word to transfer wealth to our heavenly home. Every time we freely give to the Lord, He is faithful and promises to literally store up and keep riches for us in Heaven where we can enjoy them forever. Luke 12:33 says, "Sell that ye have, and give alms; provide yourselves bags which wax not old, a treasure in the heavens that faileth not, where no thief approacheth, neither moth corrupteth."

In order to enjoy such treasures, we must act today, as it is our only opportunity. We cannot "lay up" for ourselves treasures after this life is over.

A Practical Plan

The question then comes: how can we prepare for all three points of life at the same time?

Well, we must first take off our owner's hat, and put on our manager's hat, remembering that we are managers for God's resources which He has entrusted to us. Only then can we rightly begin balanced planning for all three time frames simultaneously.

Now, imagine having three storage bins in front of you. With an imaginary marker, write the word "Forever" on the first, "The Present" on the second, and "Later in Life" on the third.

The most efficient way to assure that each "bin" receives an appropriate contribution is to make deposits to each upon receiving your income.

Honoring the Lord with the first fruits means that we are making deposits in our eternal account. We can trust God. Second Corinthians 9:10 promises that "he that ministereth seed to the sower" (God) can "minister bread for your food, and multiply your seed sown, and increase the fruits of your righteousness." Furthermore Philippians 4:17 tells us that He does all of this while making fruit "abound to your account" in Heaven.

To make appropriate contributions to your other two bins—the Present and Later in Life accounts—you'll need the savings value that you identified in the previous chapter. This is a good starting point. In the next chapter, we will walk through an exercise that helps "recapture" dollars that are escaping your family's wealth today through credit card debt. (If you do not have credit card debt, this helpful exercise can still help you increase the savings dollars added to these two accounts.)

Let's say you identified $500 in your household income to designate for savings. You could split that amount in half, contributing $250 a month for present savings and $250 a month for later in life savings.

I would suggest you consider an online bank with automatic deposit arrangements from your checking account. There are two specific reasons to do this with a different bank online. First, it is convenient. If you have to physically go into a bank and wait in line to make a savings deposit, it is easy to skip it now and then. Second, your savings account at your regular bank is conveniently connected to your household checking account, providing plenty of temptation to simply transfer funds making spending that much easier.

Make a decision that this is important to you (both of you if you are married), and make it automatic. Adding to your present day savings account is a healthy life-long process. However, there may come a time, hopefully, when you have more than you need in your present day savings.

How can you have too much in savings? Remember, the purpose for the present day savings account is to provide for the inevitable unexpected expenses and for planned, future large purchases. It is not intended as a place to have your money grow. In fact, as I write this, banks in the United States are paying less than .25 percent per year on savings accounts. When your balance grows to the point where you feel that you have enough to cover the biggest expense you may possibly face in one year (e.g. a roof may cost $10,000 to replace), you then can agree on reasonable new amounts, taking the difference (amount saved) and putting those dollars to work for you using methods we will review in the next two chapters. If and when you need to spend the money saved in your present day savings account, begin "refilling" this bin.

With the other $250 (of the $500 identified) a month, you prudently invest long-term. Many employers offer a 401(k) plan and may match the contributions that are made into this retirement account. This can be a great benefit and a means by which to accelerate the accumulation of savings for later in life. Hypothetically, you could contribute $250 a month and your employer matches that with $250 a month, thus adding $500 a month to your long-term savings! If your employer-sponsored savings or retirement plan does not offer to match your contributions, you will find that there are many benefits to investing outside of the company plan, among which are greater freedom of choice of investing options and more control in what and how you invest. Every company-sponsored plan has only a limited number investment options to choose from, which have been predetermined by the employer and the investment company that is managing the plan.

Please keep in mind that while investing in equities (stocks and mutual funds) may potentially be very rewarding, it also involves risk, which can be managed through education, discipline and rational thinking. As this is not a "How to Invest" book, be sure to seek godly counsel before making investing decisions. As these dollars are resources entrusted to you by the Giver of all things, you need wisdom and prudence when investing.

Each family's dollar amounts are going to differ, but the principles are the same. For the family that currently has no savings and desires to start, it may be beneficial to temporarily direct all of their savings dollars toward the present day, until they have a modest sum that can cover some of the more common expenses that arise, like a flat tire, a broken window in the house, or a veterinarian visit.

After you have reached a comfortable balance, then split that monthly amount and start your later-in-life fund.

Here is a diagram that shows how these three "bins" add up (values are hypothetical):

Eternity	Now	Later in Life
Tithes/Offerings	$250/month	$250/month
Treasures and Rewards	$15,000* after 5 years.	$19,247.45* after 5 years. Then add $250 per month from the "Now" bin: $143,939.51* after 10 more years

*Assumption based on annualized returns of 9% in the "Later in Life" account and 0% return in the "Now" account.

While it is wise and honorable to plan for today *and* tomorrow, we must always trust in the Lord and *not* our savings. Proverbs 23:5 says, "Wilt thou set thine eyes upon that which is not? for riches certainly make themselves wings; they fly away as an eagle toward heaven."

Hold your savings accounts loosely, and be willing to obey the voice of the Owner should He lay on your heart to give out of those funds. A friend of mine who was a faithful servant went home to be with the Lord this year. In addition to his faithful service, I happen to know that there were occasions, as he sensed the prompting of the Holy Spirit, when he gave sacrificially of his later-in-life funds. I know for certain that at this moment, being face to face with our Saviour, that he has no regret about doing that. In addition to his rewards in Heaven, the fruit of his giving is still being multiplied today. The buses that his giving helped purchase are still bringing children from the inner city to church to learn about the love of God, and the buildings which his giving helped build still provide a place for the lost to hear the gospel!

With eternity in mind, let us plan wisely for today and tomorrow, but be willing to yield our plans to His plans. His ways are good, His promises are true, His yoke is easy, and His rewards are eternal!

Chapter Eleven
Christians and Credit Cards

Debt is a scourge in America—shared among unbelievers and believers alike. Because many have "sown" debt, they have "reaped" bondage. Carrying a load of debt can bring increased stress, increased tension between spouses, and for some, feelings of despair. Needless to say, having additional credit card and other debt payments to make each month means that one is less free to give to the Lord's work. As a result, the person who is a slave to debt misses out on manifold blessings and joy that come from honoring God in the area of finances. Let's take a closer look at what causes many folks to get buried in debt.

Today it is all too common for young people right out of high school to receive "pre-approved" credit card solicitations. These credit card companies know exactly what they are doing. Appeal to the young person's pride and ego, and give them unbridled access to obtain their heart's desires without the apparent "pain" of having to wait and save up for a desired purchase. With reckless abandon, they begin to spend.

It doesn't take long for them to reach their credit limit, and, the more the cardholder owes, the more interest the lender will make. Just a small lapse in tracking purchases, and the card holders find themselves over the limit, which means they now incur a myriad of additional fees. On top of that, with new legislation, increased rates of interest can go as high as 39 percent! What started out fun has now resulted in bondage.

While many credit card users will not mirror the young person in this example, the statistics still scream of American's fascination and obsession with credit:

- Average credit card debt per household with credit card debt is $15,799.[1]
- About 50 percent of households headed by someone between 55 and 64 carry credit card

---

1   Calculated by dividing the total revolving debt in the U.S. ($793.1 billion as of May 2011 data, as listed in the Federal Reserve's July 2011 report on consumer credit) by the estimated number of households carrying credit card debt (50.2 million).

debt. And 37 percent of those headed by someone between 65 and 74 carry credit card debt.[2]

- As household wealth has declined in the downturn, more American families are facing financial distress due to high debt burdens. In 2007, before the recession began, 14.7 percent of U.S. families had debt exceeding 40 percent of their income.[3]
- Forty-one percent of cardholders from the ages of 18 to 29 made only the minimum required payment on a credit card in some of the last 12 months.[4, 5]

In its truest form, the use of a credit card is borrowing with the promise to repay, with compound interest, within a period of time. The national average default rate as of January 2012 stood at 28.6 percent, up from 27.9 percent two years earlier. The median rate also jumped, from 28.9 percent to 29.4 percent.[6]

---

2   Federal Reserve, "Survey of Consumer Finances," February 2009.

3   U.S. Congress' Joint Economic Committee, "Vicious Cycle: How Unfair Credit Card Company Practices Are Squeezing Consumers and Undermining the Recovery," May 2009.

4   FINRA Investor Education Foundation, "Financial Capability in the United States," December 2009.

5   Daniel P. Ray and Yasmin Ghahremani "Credit card statistics, industry facts, debt statistics" (Updated January 13, 2014), http://www.creditcards.com/credit-card-news/credit-card-industry-facts-personal-debt-statistics-1276.php#Credit-card-debt.

6   As reported in CreditCards.com survey of one hundred leading credit cards, January 2012).

With interest rates this high and the average cardholder paying only the "minimum" payment, is it any surprise that most people in this position are resigned to being in debt for twenty or more years? The majority of consumer debt is created by purchasing items that one is not prepared to purchase with cash. The focus on "minimum monthly payment" is the gateway to indebtedness for many people. That $50 a month doesn't seem like much, but it adds up, and soon people find themselves in over their heads.

In one's right mind (meaning when you are not in the store drooling over that seventy-inch High Definition television), would you and your spouse really believe that it is reasonable to purchase a $2,000 television at a real cost of $4,750 over a period of sixteen years? Chances are the answer is "No." Yet that is what it would actually cost your family at 13.99 percent interest, paying the minimum of $59 a month.

The retail world has made an art form out of promoting their wares in the form of monthly payments. Sales experts refer to this as "the reduction to the ridiculous." A computer with a price tag of $1,200 may be advertised as "Own this computer for only $29 a month!" By getting you to focus on the monthly payment and not the full price, they entice more buyers. This creates a mindset that costly items can be easily obtained with small monthly payments. Yet by paying only these minimum payments, a buyer is setting himself up for years of indebtedness, possibly as many as twenty years.

Many times people rationalize this by planning to pay more than the minimum, but while that is a noble intention, the reality is that unplanned expenses and changes occur in life, and when they do, we're back to paying those minimum payments. Even worse, a financial crisis such as a cut in pay or a job loss may lead to the inability to make the payments at all, leading to late fees, over-the-limit fees, and a negative credit score.

Beliefs dictate behavior

I believe that many money mistakes can be avoided without having to learn lessons the hard way—if our beliefs about money are what they should be. Our behavior will flow from our beliefs.

For example, if someone believes that traffic laws exist for our safety, that person will abide by those laws. If someone believes that drinking three cups of coffee a day will stimulate the thinking process and make him "more alert," he is likely to drink his fill of coffee.

This same principle holds true when it comes to credit card use. Notice these examples:

- If someone believes that a credit card is a means of obtaining things that he otherwise cannot afford, he will act on his belief and continue to an unhealthy practice of accruing debt.

- If someone says that a credit card is for emergencies, and if "emergencies" seem to pop up regularly in the form of a great sale at the department store, this person's belief will keep him trapped in the bondage of debt based on what he believes an "emergency" is.

- If someone believes that a particular color ("Gold" or "Platinum") of credit card or brand ("American Express") brings with it status or feeds one's self esteem, this belief may lead to spending more to gain the next level of status.

- If someone believes that the amount of credit extended to you is an affirmation of your financial standing, he may be deceived into the dangerous practice of trying to raise that limit. Creating this mentality is an art mastered by the companies that extend this credit with the goal of keeping you striving for the next card "brand" and the next credit limit increase.

I am not saying it is never proper to use a credit card. Electricity can kill you, but it makes life much more comfortable. The key with both electricity and credit cards is keeping them contained so that they do not cause damage. Compare these two lists regarding credit cards.

Destructive Use
- Believing the credit limit equals spending limit
- Using credit to obtain something you cannot presently afford
- Making purchases based on affording the minimum payment
- Paying only the minimum required monthly payment
- Paying late and incurring costly and unnecessary fees
- Going over the credit limit, thus paying extraordinary fees and triggering an increase in interest rate

Favorable Use
- Using a credit card to secure/reserve airline tickets, hotels, car rentals, etc.

- Paying off modest purchases in the next "billing cycle," avoiding finance charges and benefiting from fraud protection
- If a large balance already exists, paying more than the minimum payment per month to decrease finance charges and expedite the elimination of the debt balance
- Closing the account when paid off, leaving only one card for reserving travel and such matters
- Seeing credit cards for the source of bondage that they can be and eliminating the source of temptation

What the Bible says about borrowing

Of course the term *credit card* is not found in Scripture, but principles involving debt and borrowing abound…and they sound a clear warning about debt.

We've already looked at Proverbs 22:7: "The rich ruleth over the poor, and the borrower is servant to the lender."

The Hebrew word for *servant* used here is *ebed*, which translated means "slave." What a thought! We become slave to the lending company until our debt obligation is satisfied. They set the terms. They can increase the payments. They may be able to call the loan due. They can increase the interest rate. *Slave* is not a comforting term, yet that is the position we put ourselves in when we become indebted to a lending company. If we thought about that Bible truth, we would be far less eager to take on another low monthly payment and go further into debt.

By choosing not to be in debt in exchange for owning an item, one chooses to be free of debt bondage. If we practice delayed gratification when it comes to purchases—saving up to pay for something in full—we will avoid bondage, improve our testimony, eliminate stress, and ideally find ourselves in a better position to serve the Lord as He leads us to give.

A remedy for existing debt

The first step to getting out of debt is to have the right thinking about credit. When we view it as God does, then we are ready for the right plan. If someone still sees a credit card as a means of purchasing a desired item in the absence of real money, he will continue to struggle with destructive credit card patterns and will likely continue to stay in the destructive cycles of debt.

Many times people set out to get out of debt, only to find themselves failing. There is a dangerous pattern that brings with it the feeling of defeat, frustration, and futility. Often that pattern goes something like this:

- Excitement over the plan or remedy to finally get out of debt, but the proper view of what credit cards are, and can do is lacking.
- The plan is laid out, light appears at "the end of the tunnel."
- A payment or two is made on the targeted debt to be eliminated.
- A temptation surfaces or an "opportunity" arises and the credit card is used again.
- Rationalization that this purchase will be paid off next month, when finances "will be better"
- Next month comes along with the reality that the "extra" money to pay for that purchase is not there because something came up.
- Feelings of defeat and frustration support the wrong belief that no progress is being made so, why try?

This does not have to be your story. Thousands and thousands of people have succeeded in eliminating their credit card debt and are living in freedom as a result. Get your thinking right, and then follow a plan to get to where God wants you to be.

Here is a practical guide to paying off your credit cards.

Suggested remedies

You need to understand up front that winning the war on credit cards will generally involve being uncomfortable for a period of time, but is well worth it. The problem with this plan is not that it won't work, but rather that it requires sacrifice. To accelerate the elimination of your credit card balances, it will be a necessity to "recapture" some extra dollars in your financial picture that quite often are not accounted for. Some areas that you may look at:

- Daily coffee purchases
- Dining out
- Movie rentals/music downloads
- Multiple cell phones

Go through the budgeting process described earlier to find areas in your budget where you can reduce spending to free up money to apply toward increasing your credit card payments each month. If cutting back on those things does not generate the funds that you need to make a significant impact on your debt, consider these options:

- Cancel cable/satellite TV for a period of time
- Cancel club memberships
- Join a carpool

By applying even an additional $50 to $100 a month, you can accelerate the reduction of your balances in a fraction of the time it would otherwise take. Obviously, the more you can apply toward this goal, the faster you will reach it.

Action steps

1. Stop using credit cards completely. This can be a difficult choice. But remember, the beliefs and actions that brought you into debt will not bring you out.

2. Choose the card with the *lowest* balance, and apply the money you found in your budget earlier (perhaps $50, as an example) above the minimum monthly payment on that card each month.

    Let's take an account with a balance of $500 and a minimum monthly payment of $13. When you add $50 to the minimum payment of $13, you pay a total of $63 each month. By adding this $50 to the principle of the debt, this card will be paid off in about nine months, rather than the nine years it would take while making the minimum payments! (Of course, close this account as soon as it is paid off.)

    Some people think it would be better to begin this step on the card with the highest balance rather than the lowest balance. In many cases, the card with a higher balance has a higher interest rate as well. However, I still advise people to begin with the lowest card. There are two reasons for this. First, it gives you a quicker victory, thus boosting your confidence and resolve to continue this effort of ridding your life of consumer debt once and for all. Second, as we'll see in step 4, it allows you to more quickly create a snowball effect toward the balance of other cards.

3. While you add to your payments on your lowest card, continue to make the minimum monthly payments on time on your other card balances.

    You do not want to go further in debt by incurring additional fees.

4. Once your lowest card is paid off, target your card with the next lowest balance, and add to the current minimum payment everything you were paying on the previous card.

    Let's say that Card 2 carries an outstanding debt of $1,200 and a minimum payment of $39. You will now add to your monthly payment on Card 2 everything you were paying on the now-paid-off Card 1—which is $63. This second card can be paid off in approximately thirteen months, compared with eight to fifteen years (depending on interest rate) at the minimum payment. (Once again, close this account after it is paid off.)

5. Continue this compounding of monthly payments with the remaining cards, adding your "accelerated" payment to the minimum payment of the next card, until all is paid off.

It is a tremendous help to stay disciplined in your commitment to be free of debt when you can see the whole plan easily mapped out, and you can have a specific date for the final payment of your debt. Depending on the amount of your debt, you may be completely free in months rather than years. It is much easier to stay motivated while you work toward a short-term goal.[7]

A celebration (using cash, of course!) is absolutely appropriate when you've paid your final card off and have gained your freedom from debt!

---

7   Visit strivingtogether.com/downloads/debt-spreadsheet to download a free debt elimination spreadsheet.

Conclusion

In these pages, we've seen that our faith and finances are tightly woven together. We must never forget that God is the owner of everything and that He will hold us accountable for how we use the resources He has entrusted to us. I encourage you to use your money wisely both to provide for your family in this life and to lay up treasures in Heaven as you remain focused on eternity.

Remember, as we follow the principles of God's Word, we can trust the promises of God...and the God of the promises!

Visit us online

strivingtogether.com

wcbc.edu